SOUTHERN STEAM
THE ISLE OF WIGHT
STEAM IN THE WEST COUNTRY
LOCOMOTIVES
NORTH EASTERN
PACIFICS
CORNWALL
RAILWAY
A PICTORIAL SURVEY
WESTERNS
DIESELS
IN ACTION
LONDON MIDLAND
STEAM
SOUTHERN
STEAM IN ACTION
2
OVER SHAP
NORTH EASTERN
STEAM LOCOMOTIVE
ALBUM
GREAT WESTERN
STEAM
IN YORKSHIRE
IN ACTION
STEAM IN SOUTH WALES
AMERICAN
STEAM
MIDLAND
STEAM NORTH OF THE BORDER
LNWR
LOCOMOTIVES
OF C. J. BOWEN COOKE
SOUTHERN
EUROPEAN
STEAM
SOUTHERN
STEAM
EUROPEAN
NARROW
GAUGE
A PICTORIAL SURVEY
GREAT WESTERN
STEAM IN DEVON
IN ACTION

THE WARSHIPS – B R CLASS 42/43 DIESEL-HYDRAULICS

THE WARSHIPS

BR CLASS 42/43 DIESEL-HYDRAULICS

H. L. FORD and N. E. PREEDY

D. BRADFORD BARTON LIMITED

Frontispiece: D809 *Champion* near Corsham at the end of the climb east from Bath with a Bristol-Paddington express in the summer of 1962. The 'Warships' may be said to have been the 'Castles' of the Western Region diesel-hydraulic era. [G. A. Richardson]

For a period of something like two years during the final run-down of steam in the far West one could regularly see 'Warships' in harness with 'Castles', 'Halls' and 'Granges'. Here, No.6824 *Ashley Grange* pilots D815 *Druid*—only three months after entering service—with the overloaded 'Royal Duchy' at Easter 1960 and is seen near Angarrack, west of Camborne, in Cornwall. [P. Q. Treloar]

 IRRC *779/25BN* *ISBN 0 85153 317 5*
printed in Great Britain by H. E. Warne Ltd, London and St. Austell
for the publishers

D. BRADFORD BARTON LTD · Trethellan House · Truro · Cornwall · England

INTRODUCTION

The origins of the D800 series of diesel-hydraulics of Western Region, later known as the 'Warship' class, lay in the V200 class of locomotives on the Deutsche Bundesbahn, which had proved themselves as efficient, reliable units in service in Germany during the early 1950s. A variety of interchangeable engines (MAN, Maybach and D-Benz) were used in these, allied to transmissions built either by Voith or Mekydro; Western Region purchased drawings and a licence, to produce a version suitably compressed for the BR standard loading gauge, utilising the same 2000 bhp (later 2200 bhp) power units carried on four axles (B-B) and weighing less than 80 tons all up. As part of the pioneer stage of WR dieselisation in the West Country, this 'recipe' offered the ideal replacements for the 'Castles' and other steam 4-6-0s in service. Three initial 2000 bhp locomotives were built at Swindon from 1956-58, comprising D800-802, and a further 2200 bhp batch of 63 locomotives with detail changes was decided upon in 1957, before these three had entered service. Swindon was selected to build thirty of these (D803-832) and an outside manufacturer, North British Locomotive Co Ltd., of Glasgow, D833-865. The Swindon series (later classified as Class 42 by BR) utilised Maybach MD 650 engines, built under licence in Britain by Bristol-Syddeley Engines coupled to Mekydro transmission units: the NBL series (later forming Class 43) had NBL MAN engines (L12V18) and NBL/Voith transmission—basically Glasgow-built under licence from these German manufacturers. An exception was D830 which was fitted with two Paxman engines, to give a test to a different make of power unit.

Construction at Swindon was initially a more lengthy process than originally envisaged—partly due to the utter novelty of producing diesel-hydraulics in a works hitherto devoted solely to the building of steam locomotives and partly to a continuing loss of fitters and other skilled men to competing local industry. D800 entered service in July 1958 (officially allocated to Laira in September) followed by D801-802; and by April 1959, D803 and 804—first of the 2200 hp machines, were working in the West Country after the usual 'Warship' running-in turns on Taunton-Paddington trains. Output continued throughout the rest of 1959, 1960 and early 1961 (to February, when D832 was completed) at the rather leisurely rate of one or two a month.

Delivery of the Glasgow-built NBL series commenced with D833 arriving at Swindon in mid-June 1960, with nine into traffic by the end of that year. A further 17 followed in 1961 and the final seven in 1962, ending with D865 in June 1962. Meantime, due to impending financial troubles at NBL which were to culminate in the sad end of this world-famous locomotive builder, a further five Class 42 had been ordered from Swindon in April 1959 (D866-870) to make up the class to the full required number for Type 4s in the West of England dieselisation programme. These final Swindon five entered traffic from March-October 1961, coinciding in time more or less with the delivery of D845-855 from Glasgow.

Something of the trials and tribulations of the introduction of diesel-hydraulics on Western Region has already been touched upon in the Introduction to the sister volume to this, on the Class 52 'Westerns'. To this the interested reader is referred, for much that was applicable to these bigger six-axle diesel-hydraulics applied also to their smaller B-B 'Warship' cousins. In essence the 'Westerns' were enlarged 'Warships' with power increased to 2700 hp. Briefly speaking the main fault of the 'Warships' lay in the riding of their bogies at speed. D800 running light engine on trials near Twyford exceeded 105 mph on one occasion (in 1 minute 50 seconds from a standing start) and there was some spirited running up to 95 mph or more elsewhere in ordinary service in the early days of service but the sideways lunges of the bogies and the ensuing oscillation was reputedly enough to frighten drivers to keep down to 80 mph or less. Tests were carried out in 1959 as well as various trials; by November 1960 five of the 'Warships' were back at Swindon for attention to their bogies, so the matter was by no means rapidly cured. Curiously this trouble, and its associated bad tyre wear, had been no problem with the V200 bogies, although they did not have the severe curves of the WR South Devon route to contend with. An 80 mph speed limit was imposed on the class, although the modifications in 1960-61 enabled this to be removed later.

Engine performance of the NBL-built series was never as good as those from Swindon and they required considerably more minor repairs and maintenance. In 1966, for example, incipient engine failures were so widespread among D833-865 that a de-rating to 2000 bhp was tried for some time. Depot reports on the single high-speed Paxman engines 'variant' (D830) were good, it being found particularly light on maintenance. The West of England services were the principal preserve of the 'Warships' throughout their careers, though they also worked on the North-and-West route and to a lesser degree on the Northern Line (Paddington to the Midlands) helping out the 'Westerns'. In 1968-9, as mentioned in detail later in this volume, 'Warships' in pairs (working in multiple) were used to power selected West of England expresses on accelerated schedules, principally 'The Cornish Riviera' and some impressive runs were recorded by these 4400 bhp combinations.

The standardisation policy announced in 1967 for the BR diesel fleet of the future was the first intimation of the end of the 'Warships'. The initial three (D800-802) were withdrawn in the autumn of 1968, being then ten years old. The annual write-down in value of a 'Warship' from £120,000 or more as the price new, to a scrap value of perhaps £10,000 only a decade later, was a daunting £12,000 a year in capital lost. Against this, annual mileages were high and this factor needs to be borne in mind. The non-standard D830 was withdrawn permanently in 1969, whilst at the same period some of the Class 43s (including Nos.839 and 845) were put back into service after having spent some time stored. Nos.842 and 852 were, for example, in store at this same time at Newton Abbot, pending the introduction of surplus ex-ER Class 31s to Western Region. The rest of the two constituent classes of 'Warships' (Class 42 and 43) were withdrawn steadily during 1971, with the NBL ones—always the least satisfactory—the first to go. The bigger diesel-hydraulics had something of a reprieve as regards their planned phasing-out, due to the massive price rise of oil, and there was some considerable movement of the 'Warships' into and out of store as a result of changes in WR locomotive requirements. Their last regular duties were on Merehead to Gatwick/Merstham stone trains up to the autumn of 1972—a type of work their designers surely never envisaged for them—until replaced by 47s.

The diesel-hydraulics chapter in the story of British Railways since the end of steam is now at an end, with the last surviving 'Westerns' gone. We will continue to see a few preserved hydraulics hauling specials and at work on privately-owned lines, but an era has passed in the history of Britain's railways.

D801 *Vanguard* was the second of the three Swindon prototypes (D800-2) and went into traffic three months after pioneer D800, early in November 1958. She is seen here outside A Shop at Swindon on 17 September still in the final stages of construction and in undercoat ready for her green livery. D802 *Formidable* followed *Vanguard* into service about one month later. [M. J. Jackson]

First of the Swindon 'Warships', D800, on display in A Shop on 27 July 1958, a fortnight or so before officially going into service. This was the sole example of the class not to bear a 'Warship' or naval name (see also page 20), being named after Sir Brian Robertson who was at this period chairman of the British Transport Commission. The naming ceremony had been held at Paddington the previous month.
[Norman E. Preedy]

DANGER
D 800

D817 *Foxhound* outside Swindon Works on 18 March 1960, a week or so after starting service. At Swindon eleven 'Warships' were built in 1959 (D803-813), and sixteen (D814-829) in 1960, followed by eight in 1961 (D830-832 and 866-870). Detail differences are visible when comparing this photograph with D800 on the preceding pages. Fold-over discs have gone and a neater indicator panel has been fitted, together with extended grab rails to give a better grip when cleaning the screens. Additional ventilation louvres have been cut amidships in the roof to reduce the temperature inside around the train heating boiler. The panel fairing over the fueltank fillers has also been dispensed with.

[Norman E. Preedy]

The D800 'Warships' were the first major class to be used in implementing dieselisation in the West Country, Cornwall and Devon having been chosen as the pioneer area for the introduction of the new type of motive power on Western Region. On 23 September 1959, D800 *Sir Brian Robertson* shows the look of things to come as the driver notches up towards full power shortly after leaving Penzance with the up 'Cornish Riviera'. It was recorded that the first working of D800 on the 'Riviera' was on 15 July 1958, from Paddington as far as Plymouth during road trials prior to officially entering service. [P. Q. Treloar]

D801 *Vanguard* eases the 'Cornish Riviera' past the motive power depot to the stop at Truro on a morning in July 1959. By this date there were nine of the class in service, plus the five A1A-A1A 'Warships' (D600-4), all of them allocated to Laira depot at Plymouth. [P. Q. Treloar]

D807 *Caradoc* arrived new at Laira from Swindon Works late in June 1959 and is seen here near Hayle with the 10.05 Penzance - Manchester the following month. She will probably work this train only as far as Plymouth, being still regarded as running-in and in any event would not proceed at this period beyond Bristol. [P. Q. Treloar]

D800 at Temple Meads, Bristol, in 1960 with 'The Bristolian' headboard up. The new diesel-hydraulics first worked this prestige express on 16 February 1959 and put up some fine performances, enabling the start-to-stop average to be raised to more than 70 mph for the first time. Speeds of more than 100 mph were recorded on occasion, until an overall limit was imposed. [P. Heywood]

Odd man out amongst the 'Warships' was D830 *Majestic* which had two 1200 bhp Paxman 12YJXL engines installed in place of the standard Maybach ones. She entered traffic in January 1961, allocated to Newton Abbot, and is seen here at Temple Meads a few months later. [P. Heywood]

COMPASS

IF 47

D800 slams through Newbury with a down West of England express on a wet day in August 1959. Below, D832 *Onslaught* piloting 'Castle' Class No.7001 *Sir James Milne* near Westbourne Park with the 14.55 Paddington - Bristol and Swansea, 17 May 1961. [D. Fereday Glenn]

D841 *Roebuck,* seen here at Reading in 1961, was one of the NBL-built 'Warships', turned out the preceding January. Identifying the two series externally was difficult apart from the names—the Swindon ones A to O, those from Glasgow P-Z, apart from the extra final five Z ones additionally built by Swindon. [C. J. Blay]

D 801

1C31

No.6869 *Resolven Grange* and D805 *Benbow* team up with a down Penzance express, 8 July 1961, and are seen on the speed restricted curve at Chacewater, west of Truro. Steam and diesel doubleheading was an undesirable but unavoidable feature of operations westward from Newton Abbot in the busy summer seasons of the early 1960s. [M. J. Messenger]

aira had enough 'Warships' to add the 'Torbay Express' into the new diesel diagrams late in July 1959, ringing D800 and her sisters to Kingswear for the first time. Here, D801 *Vanguard* has charge of the up xpress at Churston on 5 August of that year, an interloper on the South Devon steam scene.
[J. R. Besley]

hird to be built of the NBL series, D835 *Pegasus* passing Dawlish Warren with the down 'Cornish iviera' on 1 October 1960, some two months after entering service. [W. L. Underhay]

Early in their career the 'Warships' were rare on freight turns, the first of these not being incorporated in the Laira diagrams until about March 1960. Here D841 *Roebuck* has a Class 6 freight at Aller Junction bound for Plymouth, 29 September 1961. Banking in the rear is a 63xx NBL, which will help up Dainton. Operational rules at this date were that approximately one third of the wagons in any mainline freight worked by diesel-hydraulics had to be vacuum-brake fitted. The 'Warships' were of course intended primarily for express passenger work and their lack of weight for braking power always effectively precluded their use on loose-coupled freights. In this instance, the necessity for a banking locomotive is dictated not by the haulage capacity of the 'Warship', but by regulations governing the working of unbraked freight trains on rising gradients. [W. L. Underhay]

D827 *Kelly* between Teignmouth and Newton Abbot with the down 'Torbay Expres
July 1961. This was a standard 'Warship' duty for almost a decade. [W. L. Underha

D820 *Grenville* with an up milk train for Kensington on 14 October 1961, photographed at the entrance to Dainton Tunnel.
[W. L. Underhay]

Sea mist shrouds Torquay station on a March morning in 1961 as D812 waits for the right-away with the up 'Torbay Express'. This was the odd man out in the main 'Warships' naming sequence, due to a last minute decision to change the name from *Despatch* to *The Royal Naval Reserve 1859-1959.* This was to honour the centenary of the latter body, the nameplate being unveiled in a ceremony held at Paddington in November 1959. D812 was the last to be turned out with the old style of folding discs to show head codes, D813 having the new four-digit illuminated panels. The A68 reporting code seen here on the 'Torbay Express' is in fact formed from separate removable panels as also concurrently used in frames on the smoke box front of WR steam locomotives. [J. R. Besley]

D856 *Trojan,* built in November 1961, growls her way up the adverse grades of Brewham bank near Bruton with a thirteen coach express on 1 June 1963. The first main sphere of operations of the 'Warships' for their initial three years of service was between Paddington - Bristol and Paddington - Penzance. North or west of Bristol they were rare until 1962—although D800 had made a run through to Cardiff back in July 1958 'flying the flag' on a special. Partly this was due to lack of trained crews and of re-fuelling points, plus the fact that this was after all their designated sphere of operations. [G. A. Richardson]

A broadside view of D849 *Superb* entering Paddington on 3 June 1961 with a West of England express, a few days after acceptance by Swindon from NBL works. With their MAN/Voith engine transmissions, the NBL series weighed 80 tons in working order with full tanks, almost two tons more than the Swindon-built Maybach-Mekydro ones. Fuel capacity at 800 gallons was the same in them all, plus 940 gallons water for the train heating boiler. [D. Fereday Glenn]

D842 *Royal Oak* entering Redruth station with a down train from Penzance, 30 July 1961. She is in the standard original Brunswick green livery with pale grey body stripe. The removable roof panels, originally painted a darker shade of grey, are now effectively black after some months of service. [M. J. Messenger]

An improvised four-figure reporting code decorates the front end of D807 *Caradoc* on 12 May 1962, seen here shortly after crossing Moorswater Viaduct at Liskeard with a Sheffield-Penzance train. By this date, all but the last of the 'Warships' had been built, with only D865 *Zealous* still to come from Glasgow. [M. J. Messenger]

An unusual location to see 'Warships' in 1961 was Exeter (Central) for it was another three years before they were to be used regularly on Southern lines. On this occasion, on 26 August, a landslip at Lavington caused a diversion from the WR main line. D818 *Glory* (above) is coming in with the 9.30 a.m. Paddington-Newquay and D852 *Tenacious* (below) is seen passing Exeter (St. James' Park) with the 9.20 up from St. Ives. [W. L. Underhay]

IC 28
IA 75
ST. JAMES PARK
HALT

D824 *Highflyer* at Newton Abbot diesel shed, 17 March 1962. Initially this depot had been chosen as the principal one in the area for main line diesels to operate from but subsequently it was decided instead to develop Laira (Plymouth) as the principal maintenance depot. After Laira had received the first dozen or so of the class, others went new to Newton Abbot and later on the latter was to have a monopoly of them, with the bigger 'Westerns' based solely on Laira. This sensible concentration scheme helped the stocking of spares and enabled the maintenance staff and the drivers to become 100 per cent familiar with all the requirements and foibles of each. [Norman E. Preedy]

Contrasts at Paddington; D832 *Onslaught,* last of the main Swindon order, beside No.6001 *King Edward VII,* 17 June 1961. Even with the stringent weight saving that had been necessary with the diesel-hydraulics, the weight of the former with full tanks came to only ten tons or so less than the massively built King without its trailing tender. Tractive effort of the two types was fairly comparable. Route classification of the 'Warship' was 'Red', compared to 'Double Red' of the 'King' with its 22½ ton axle load. [C. L. Caddy]

The G & S W R route via Kilmarnock to Dumfries and Carlisle was used for the initial road tests of D833 etc from 1960-62, as it had been earlier for their predecessors the D600 'Warships'. This is another unidentifiable member of the class, photographed at Dumfries on a trial run. [J. H. Court]

One of the N B L-built 'Warships', carrying no number or name, at Glasgow undergoing preliminary trials prior to despatch to Swindon for acceptance by Western Region. [J. H. Court]

1V73

D824 *Highflyer* followed D829 in pioneering the first SR West of England 'Warship'-hauled services and is seen here passing Seaton Junction with the 11.30 Brighton-Plymouth on 8 August 1964. It had taken this over at Salisbury. On the left No.34105 *Swanage* is shunting milk tanks in the creamery sidings. To make driver training easier, only Swindon-built 'Warships' were initially used on SR territory, excluding the 2000 hp initial trio as well as D830 with its Paxman engines plus D818 which had a different train heating boiler. [W. L. Underhay]

The Swindon-built series of 'Warships' extended their sphere of operations on to Southern Region in the summer of 1964, with D829 *Magpie* sent to Salisbury for crew training (initially on trains to and from Basingstoke) in June. In August test runs were made between Waterloo and Exeter in preparation for these diesels to take over from the Bulleid Pacifics which were by this date getting into a somewhat rundown condition. Late in August a 'Warship' hauled the 'Atlantic Coast Express' but alas no photograph of this is known and this scene is of D807 *Caradoc* on the 3 p.m. Waterloo-Exeter near Basingstoke on 19 March 1966. 'Warships' were a great success on this change-over of the Exeter-Waterloo trains to a two-hourly semi-fast service. In comparing this photograph with page 12, it can be seen that the newer-style four character headcode panel has replaced the original style carried by D807 in its early years. A yellow warning panel has also been added. [Norman E. Preedy]

IV71
D 823

A close-up of D823 *Hermes* at Basingstoke with a Waterloo-Exeter train, June 1966. Note the ship's crest of the 'Warship' after which she was named affixed below the cab window. Other points of interest are the 84A (Laira) shed plate and the additional footstep at the front end below the buffer which was a later fitting to the class. A stencilled letter on the doorhandle recess indicates the A end. The locomotive is seen here with the small yellow warning panel round the headcode panel first introduced late in 1961, and also carries maroon livery, a newer BR 'coaching stock' crest, and has lost the distinctive bodyside white stripe carried by green-liveried locomotives.
[Norman E. Preedy]

D838 *Rapid* outside Swindon Works, 20 May 1962, exhibits the familiar diamond-shaped NBL builder's plate on the solebar amidships. [Norman E. Preedy]

D822 *Hercules* alongside Hymek D7026 in Swindon Works, 6 October 1963, shows th
considerable difference in appearance between the rounded lines of the 'Warship' fro
end and the more deliberately styled Beyer Peacock design. [David Bulloc

D841 *Roebuck* in the works after overhaul in July 1965. She is still in the original 'Warship' livery of Brunswick green which suited the class so well—particularly after the small yellow panel had been added—but later the same year they began to appear from the paint shop in the radically different maroon livery. The story of 'Warship' liveries is a rather complex one, with 32 of the class repainted from green to maroon from mid 1965 to early 1967 but four (D826, 837, 850 and 860) also outshopped in this same period in green.
[P. Heywood]

The rounded front end of the 'Warships' seemed to weather badly as regards the surface finish, and thereafter grew more and more ingrained with dirt. This is very evident in this frontal view of D867 *Zenith* easing into St. Austell station on 4 July 1970 with a down train. She was the second of the final batch of five built by Swindon, entering traffic in April 1961. [Norman E. Preedy]

How a 'Warship' should look! D809 *Champion* on 30 May 1963 at Reading with No.7011 *Banbury Castle* on a down express for Plymouth. She exhibits a combination of yellow warning panel around the original style of three removable train number panels. [D. Williams]

D826 *Jupiter* has power off as she coasts towards Teignmouth on a June morning in 1967 with the 10.35 Exeter-Kingswear. [G. F. Gillham]

Later the same day, D848 *Sultan* passes the same location with the up 'Devonian' (Kingswear-Bradford), immaculate in maroon livery. This colour was originally chosen for the 'Westerns' as the result of a public opinion poll, and later extended to the 'Warships' as a standardisation measure; no other diesel classes varied from a green livery, and one saw only green Deltics, BR-Sulzer, English Electric and Brush Type 4s, as well as Hymeks, etc, until 'Rail Blue' livery came in during the 1964-6 period. Fortunately the 'Warships' looked well in either colour, although the dark green seemed more appropriate to a Swindon product. [G. F. Gillham]

1N05

Maroon liveried D829 *Magpie* on 20 August 1967 photographed on the climb away from Wilton at the head of the 11.00 Waterloo - Exeter. The train is a curious mixture of BR standard and SR Bulleid coaching stock, marshalled in alternating fashion. [G. F. Gillham]

D828 *Magnificent* belies her name as she stands in the loco bay at Salisbury with Class 33 D6532 on a January day in 1969. The works-applied small yellow panel shows up in contrast with the very worn coat of yellow paint applied subsequently at a local maintenance depot to meet the later requirements of BR. Below, D824 *Highflyer* entering Yeovil Junction with an up train on 9 July 1968. The O forming the second letter of the headcode indicates a through train from the WR to the Southern; down trains would have a V in this position. [G. F. Gillham]

MAGNIFICENT
D828
7F08
REFRESHMENTS
1012

D803 *Albion* on the 10.55 a.m. Plymouth - Brighton passing Yeoford, 3 October 1964. The 'Warships' used on the Southern continued to be on WR strength, and based on either Laira or Newton Abbot shed. They were also seen on services to Weymouth occasionally, as well as on the SR Plymouth - Exeter route via Okehampton as seen here. [C. L. Caddy]

D848 *Sultan* about to leave Penzance with the up 'Cornishman'; the locomotive would work as far as Bristol in this instance. Up to the spring of 1962 the class did not work north or west of Bristol but from March onwards of that year they commenced to run over the North and West route via Shrewsbury to Crewe. Newton Abbot's celebrated double-homer turns for its 'Castles', out and back to Shrewsbury, became a regular 'Warship' roster, with fill-in turns from there to Crewe and back. The electric warning flashes, reminding crews of the danger of overhead electrified lines, were fitted about this time as a result of this extension of 'Warship' territory into Crewe. A later addition to 'Warship' workings was the Paddington-Oxford-Worcester services; this was the province of Class 43s allocated to Old Oak Common. [Cecil J. Blay]

From March 1968 Western Region instituted the use of a pair of 'Warships' in multiple to enable an accelerated West of England service to be given with selected expresses. A dozen or so of the Class 42s had their m.u. couplings replaced (after these had earlier been removed) and the sight of 4400 hp on the head end of the 'Cornish Riviera' became standard for a time. The South Devon banks were made very short work of, and extremely rapid recoveries could of course be made after any signal checks or other delays. Here D822 *Hercules* and D829 *Magpie* are racing along near Hungerford in July 1968.

[D. E. Canning]

The up 'Cornish Riviera' with fourteen coaches on at Grafton behind one of the pairs of 'Warships' diagrammed for this working. In 1969 the separation and increased frequency of the Cornwall and Torbay services, and the consequent reduction in the numbers of coaches per train, meant that the 2700 hp 'Westerns' could handle the loads involved and as a result only the 'Riviera' remained a regular 'twin-Warship' duty. There were two pairs in regular Laira diagrams in 1969 with a pair doing over 1500 miles in each 48 hour period to special timing. [D. E. Canning]

The standardisation of monastral or rail blue livery with full yellow ends was introduced by BR in the mid 1960s, and in the summer of 1966 'Warships' first appeared in this new style. The all-yellow end, carried up above the windscreen, made a considerable change in their overall appearance which some lineside observers felt was not an improvement. In 1966 also the new BR logo replaced the former emblem, being re-positioned first beneath the numbers at each end, and later amidships on each side below the nameplate and not above. From 1968 onwards the D prefix to the cabside number was also deleted—all these external changes being exemplified here by No.820 *Grenville,* seen after general overhaul and full repaint at Swindon in August 1971. [Norman E. Preedy]

The enlarged development of the 'Warship' was, of course, the equally well known 'Western' class of 2700 hp, utilising the same diesel-hydraulic formula using German-designed essentials but carried on six axles. When completion of the last 'Warship' of all, D870 *Zulu,* was nearing completion in the autumn of 1961, work had already started alongside on D1000, first of the 'Westerns'. Together with the Beyer-Peacock Hymek Type 3s these two diesel-hydraulic classes provided the backbone of the first decade of Western Region's change-over to diesel traction. Here, No.832 *Onslaught* is alongside a 'Western' in the stabling point at Exeter (St. Davids) in what was formerly the steam shed there, 29 May 1971. [Norman E. Preedy]

812
870

Last of the class, No.870 *Zulu,* in the loco sidings at Exeter, May 1971. Overall length over buffers was 60′, and 37′9″ between bogie pivot centres (wheelbase 10′6″). Fuel tanks and batteries are carried behind the skirts between the bogies. The seven removable roof panels can be seen as standard on all 'Warships' whilst the small fairing at each end of the roof cover the air horns which on No.870 alone were not mounted in the standard position low down beneath the buffer beams. D870 also differed in other details and was initially intended to be equipped for electric train heating but the components for this were in fact removed before the locomotive went into service.
[Norman E. Preedy]

808
D 827
KELLY
D 827
D 7057

No.808, bereft of her nameplate *Centaur,* a few weeks after withdrawal in November 1971. Below, D827 *Kelly* moving away from Bristol (Bath Road) depot in October 1969. Note the BR emblem is carried on the cab sides. [Norman E. Preedy]

D834 *Pathfinder* seen at Gloucester on 20 March 1970 still retains the old livery, BR 'lion and wheel' emblem and even a red route classification disc below the number, but has had all-yellow ends added. [Norman E. Preedy]

1V19
D804

D804 *Avenger,* August 1971. The small stencil behind the door reads Laira 84A, a replacement for the old style shedplate which had evidently recently been removed from the skirt by the nearside buffer.
[Norman E. Preedy]

No.858 *Valorous* soon after withdrawal in October 1971. The NBL machines (Class 43) were the first 'Warships' to be taken out of service, being withdrawn in batches during 1971 apart from the initial three (840/848/863) withdrawn in 1969. First of the Swindon-built ones to go had been D800-802 during 1968, the non-standard D830 with Paxman engines in 1969—the rest during 1971-2.
[Norman E. Preedy]

With the impending demise of the 'Warships' in 1971-2 interest increased amongst enthusiasts and the last few members of the class to remain in service drew considerable attention. Here No.820 *Grenville* is one of the attractions at Old Oak Common depot on an Open Day in September 1972, two months or so prior to withdrawal. [Norman E. Preedy]

A close up of No.834 *Pathfinder* and No.858 *Valorous* shortly before withdrawal.
[Norman E. Preedy]

6V86
D832
Ess

D832 *Onslaught* in rather work-worn condition at Horton Road Shed, Gloucester, 29 April 1970. This 'Warship' was sent to the Derby Research Centre after withdrawal on 16 December 1972; No.818 had also been put in store, earmarked to provide 'cannibalised' spares for No.832. [Norman E. Preedy]

D836 *Powerful,* seen at Gloucester in the depot sidings with D1040 *Western Queen,* 3 March 1970. Opposite: Swindon and NBL 'Warships' at Bristol, Temple Meads—D870 *Zulu* and D846 *Steadfast* on 28 June 1969. Detail front end differences are apparent between the two, D846 having the 'cleaned-up' front with headboard clips and top lamp bracket removed and cab ventilating air inlet moved from beside the indicator panel to below the buffers; D870 exhibits its unique roof-mounted warning horns. [Norman E. Preedy]

D870
6Z19
846
6C31

The cast aluminium nameplates of the class had raised letters in a polished finish which showed up well against the red-painted (later black-painted) background. The words 'Warship Class' were carried beneath the name of all from D801 onwards except D812 *The Royal Naval Reserve 1859-1959* which occupied two lines. This illustration also shows the BR 'cycling lion' emblem above the nameplate.
[D. Bullock]

The nameplate of D821 *Greyhound,* the 'Warship' which is now preserved, as it appeared in later BR days. The oval works plate, with the wording 'BUILT 1960 SWINDON' can also be seen on the skirting covering the solebar. [G. F. Gillham]

D800 *Sir Brian Robertson* on a Sunday duty in June 1966 at Long Rock, outside Penzance, working a ballast train from Menheniot quarries. [F. Spence]

When BR divided their diesel fleet into classes, the Swindon built 'Warships' became Class 42 and those from NBL, Class 43. No.857 *Undaunted* was one of the latter, seen here on a freight in these two views at Horton Road Crossing Gloucester, and Gloucester Eastgate, on 16 October 1969. [Norman E. Preedy]

Overleaf: a study of Class 42 D866 *Zebra* with a Bristol-Old Oak Common stock and parcels train waiting for the road near Thingley Junction in October 1970. [S. Creer]

ENPARTS
D866

D866

D815 *Druid* entering Exeter (St. Davids) station with a train from Barnstaple, 31 July 1971. [Norman E. Preedy]

Paintwork on the 'Warships' seemed difficult to keep in good order—as various other illustrations in this volume show—and D832 *Onslaught,* photographed on a parcels train at Gloucester Central on 3 June 1970, appears to be in a badly run-down condition externally. [Norman E. Preedy]

D839 *Relentless,* in maroon livery with small yellow warning panel, waiting departure time at Penzance with an up express for Paddington, May 1968. [F. Spence]

No.829 *Magpie* at Paddington, 25 September 1971. Note the two diamond-shaped white markings on the buffer beam, showing that this was one of the dozen or so 'Warships' re-equipped with multiple unit controls in 1968 for double-headed workings by this class. [Norman E. Preedy]

INSURANCE
8
829
1A81

No.810 *Cockade* heading up the short branch from the Wharves at Hayle in Cornwall after shunting the sidings there on 14 July 1971. This was a fill-in trip working from Penzance and at one time frequently a 'Warship' turn. The brake van is crossing the bridge over the eastern (Copperhouse) inlet of the Hayle estuary. [South Devon Railway Museum]

No.816 *Eclipse* passing Chard Junction in the summer of 1972 with a down express. [N. L. Hawk

1V13

806
867
1B95

'Warships' at Exeter; No.806 *Cambrian* and No.867 *Zenith,* on 31 July 1971. *Zenith* is on the 7.18 a.m. Paddington-Penzance.
[Norman E. Preedy]

With its twin Maybach engines at full power and producing a sound that could be heard for some minutes before the train came into view, Class 42 No.832 *Onslaught* roars up the last stage of Dainton bank with the 09.20 Penzance-Manchester, 22 July 1972. [G. F. Gillham]

D825 *Intrepid* entering Bristol (Temple Meads) with a Paignton-Nottingham t
12 July 1969. Bath Road depot is on the left. [Norman E. Pre

Maroon-liveried D870 *Zulu* and D869 *Zest,* the last pair of the Swindon-built 'Warships', team up with the 06.10 Penzance-Paddington, 12 July 1969. The setting is Fairwood Junction. [D. H. Ballantyne]

With their relatively low all-up weight, and consequent braking ability, 'Warships' were not designed for loose-coupled freight working. Nevertheless in their later years they ran Class 8 freights in various parts of the South-West. This is No.823 *Hermes,* photographed between Radstock and Mells Road with a coal train for Frome, on 24 February 1971. [M. J. Jackson]

Class 42 No.824 *Highflyer* was one of the last four 'Warships' to remain in service, being withdrawn in December 1972. Five months before this, on 19 July, No.824 nears the top of Hemerdon bank with a lengthy train of empty ballast hoppers bound for Stoneycombe quarries. [G. F. Gillham]

With sea mist rolling in from Mounts Bay, No.839 *Relentless,* with an up parcels train from Penzance, passing the former station building at Marazion on a day in July 1971.
[South Devon Railway Museum]

No.812 *The Royal Naval Reserve 1859-1959* heading a Salisbury - Severn Tunnel Junction freight through Westbury station in March 1972. This was the 'Warship' in the main series with a non-standard name and had originally been scheduled to be named *Despatch.* [G. F. Gillham]

Class 42 No.824 *Highflyer* stabled at Westbury on 17 March 1972 prior to working a train to Weymouth. [G. F. Gillham]

In its last two months of service, No.832 *Onslaught* stands outside Newton Abbot depot on 2 September 1972. The 'Warships' had been allocated here to concentrate them for maintenance purposes and the supply of spares, with the 'Westerns' all at Laira depot, Plymouth. Up to 1971, 'Warship' allocations were split between Laira, Newton Abbot and Old Oak Common. [G. F. Gillham]

9P33
1952
1A59
832
ONSLAUGHT

In their final period of service the Class 42s were increasingly used on stone trains to or from Merehead quarries in Somerset, a duty which their designers certainly never envisaged. Here No.818 *Glory* heads out of Salisbury on the now-closed GWR route to Wilton with a train of stone empties from Merstham, 9 July 1972. [G. F. Gillham]

No.862 *Viking* entering Paddington with the 08.40 from Weston-super-Mare, 19 May 1971 and (below) No.864 *Zambesi* leaving Temple Meads with a Plymouth-Paddington parcels, 13 March 1971. Withdrawal of the NBL Class 43s began in earnest in that year and these two locomotives had both gone by October and late March respectively. [G. F. Gillham]

1A46
D854
M 81070

1V70

Class 42 No.804 *Avenger* on the curve away from Aller Junction with the down 'Cornishman' on 14 July 1969—a regular 'Warship' duty. Twelve well-laden coaches was a formidable load for a locomotive weighing only 78 tons all-up to handle over 1 in 37 gradients but the 'Warships' took it in their stride. 400 tons was their official standard load limit (compared to 380 tons for the D600 series and 525 tons for 'Westerns'). [G. F. Gillham]

Latterly the 'Warships' became deservedly popular as motive power for enthusiasts' specials; on 16 April 1972 the GWS and Plymouth Railway circle combined forces to run an excursion from the West Country to the 'Bluebell Line' in Sussex. This train was worked by No.821 *Greyhound* from Plymouth to Salisbury where No.810 *Cockade* is seen leaving on the second stage of the journey. [G. F. Gillham]

Devon and the 'Warships' were inseparable—Newton Abbot being latterly their main base. Here, No.868 *Zephyr* passes Aller Junction with an up NCL 'sundries' block train on 21 July 1970. By this date the D800s were frequently seen on parcels and freight traffic in the Region. [G. F. Gillham]

In its original green livery but with all-yellow ends, No.810 *Cockade* in a night scene at Salisbury station with the 18.20 Exeter-Waterloo on 29 September 1968. From the autumn of 1971 these services passed to the care of Southern Region's own Class 33s, with e.t.h. stock and limited (8-coach) loads, displacing the 'Warships' which had performed so well. [G. F. Gillham]

PLATFORM
LADIES
1018

7
IV47
82

No.821 *Greyhound* outside Laira depot at Plymouth, 29 August 1971. Withdrawn from traffic in December 1972, this was one of the last two to survive (with No.818) and it has now been preserved. As regards livery, it is interesting to note that preservation work of No.821 revealed over the years that she had received two coats of green paint, one of maroon and two of blue. [Norman E. Preedy]

1A55
1V11

Vatched by the
rossing-keeper at the
ast end of Exeter
St. Davids), No.821
ireyhound in her last
ummer of service
rings in the 12.30
'addington-Paignton,
1 July 1972. Below,
lo.827 *Kelly* in
anuary 1971 on the
ingle line section at
Vilton with a down
xpress for Exeter.
[G. F. Gillham]

A 'Warship' about to be launched! An unidentified member of the class on the 6.40 Newton Abbot – Paddington eases dead slow over a badly flooded section of the line at Thatcham.
[D. E. Canning]

A long line of withdrawn 'Warships' and D63xx NBL diesel-hydraulics at Marsh Junction sidings in Bristol. Withdrawal of the class began in earnest in 1971 during which year all the Class 43 NBL ones disappeared. Eleven Class 42s also went and in 1972 the slaughter of the remainder continued—withdrawal being basically in the order of them having been overhauled, this leaving the best until last. [Norman E. Preedy]

Nos.811 (*Daring*), 866 (*Zebra*) and 827 (*Kelly*) outside Newton Abbot depot in July 1972, some months after withdrawal, awaiting their last journey to Swindon and cutting-up. Nameplates have been removed and, as in the case of the earlier withdrawals, all other re-usable 'cannibal' items were removed. The oil price rise had earlier given a reprieve to some of the 'Warships' which were stored for a while and not condemned, in a few cases even being put back into traffic for a while. [G. F. Gillham]

More 'Warships' at Marsh Junction sidings in November 1971 awaiting onward movement to Swindon Works for scrapping. Visible are Nos.868, 819, 822, 808 and 843. Below, Nos.839, 861, 838 and 858 at Swindon, May 1972. The cutting-up of 'Warships', from 1971 onwards, was the first time locomotives had been broken up here for some years. [Norman E. Preedy]

The body shell of No.852 (*Tenacious*) in the scrap yard at Swindon, May 1972. Last of the NBLs to be cut up were Nos.838 and 839 a few months later. Below, the two dismembered cab portions of No.828 (*Magnificent*) in March 1972.
[Norman E. Preedy]

On 24 May 1973, No.821 *Greyhound* was photographed passing Taunton *en route* from Laira depot to Didcot under her own power, destined for preservation by a private owner. This was probably the last time a 'Warship' worked along the West of England main line in the diesel-hydraulic era. At one stage it had been hoped that another 'Warship' might have been saved, for use on the Dart Valley line in South Devon. Next to the last one to go had been No.818 (*Glory*) which went to Swindon from Laira in April, intended to be put in store there to provide essential spares when required for No.832, which had been sent to the Derby research centre. [J. Reeves]

STEAM IN ACTION

GREAT WESTERN
STEAM DOUBLEHEADED

SCOTTISH STEAM
IN THE 1920s

LNER STEAM

GREAT WESTERN
STEAM ON SHED

SPECIALS

INDUSTRIAL
NARROW
GAUGE
RAILWAYS
IN BRITAIN

NORTH EAST
STEAM

MORE SOUTHERN

DIESELS

BR STANDARD
BRITANNIA PACIFICS

LONDON MIDLAND
STEAM

GREAT WESTERN
STEAM IN ACTION 2

MIDLAND

SOUTHERN STEAM

SKIPTON-CARLISLE

MORE BRITISH
NARROW GAUGE
STEAM

LMSR

STEAM
H. C. CASSERLEY

AUSTRIAN STEAM

SCOTTISH

MOTIVES